When the Twinkle is Gone

A Child's Perspective on Death

Kama,

may your Twinkle shine brightly. Thank you for all your support. Beverly C

Written by Beverly Cuevas

Illustrated by Paula Pugh

When the Twinkle is Gone
A Child's Perspective on Death

Written by Beverly Cuevas
Illustrated by Paula Pugh

Book design, layout & illustration editing by Joe Menth, Fine Balance Imaging Studios.

www.fbistudios.com

For more information:
www.twinklebook.com

Printed in U.S.A.

DEDICATION

To Joan McBride and Family

This book honors Joan's bravery as she faced her death. It also honors, with the greatest of respect, her family for surrounding her goodbye with dignity and love.

INTRODUCTION

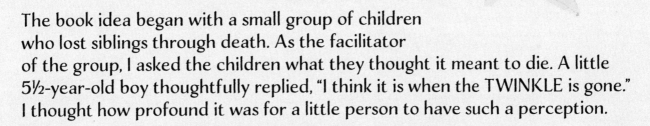

I have written this book to give recognition to
the fact that children can understand the natural
cycle of life and death. Death doesn't have to be a
frightening topic to discuss with children.

The book idea began with a small group of children
who lost siblings through death. As the facilitator
of the group, I asked the children what they thought it meant to die. A little
5½-year-old boy thoughtfully replied, "I think it is when the TWINKLE is gone."
I thought how profound it was for a little person to have such a perception.

We adults often talk about the soul, spirit, or life force as our definition of the
TWINKLE. When our TWINKLE is gone, our shell is left. That which makes us
alive is no longer present in our body.

At 5½ years, children are moving developmentally from "magical thinking" to
the realization that the dead person is not coming back.

I hope you will read on to experience for yourself and your children where
Leo believes his Nana's TWINKLE has gone.

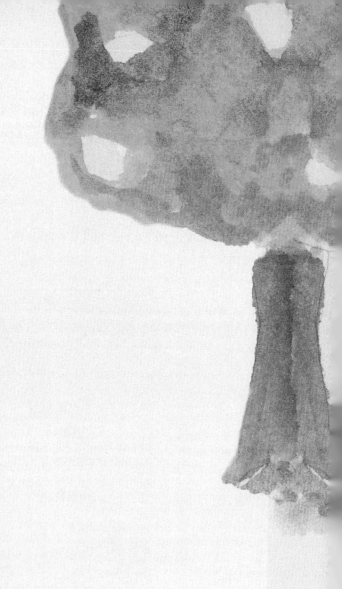

While playing in the school yard, Leo and
his friends find a little bird that is not moving.

Leo runs to school to tell the teacher what they have found.

The teacher comes out carrying
a tiny silver box, flowers, seashells,
and several heart-shaped stones.
She asks the children, "What do
you think it means to die?"

Leo pipes up, "She is not breathing. She is not moving. She is not flying.

I think her TWINKLE is gone."

The teacher and the children dig a hole under a tree full of blossoms. They gently place the little bird in the tiny silver box. They lay the box in the ground and cover it with dirt. Then they surround the grave with the flowers, seashells, and heart stones.

The children softly sing a song called "The Little Bird Is Dead"

Ring around the rosie, the little bird is dead.
Pick a pack of posies, put flowers 'round her head.
Gather up some seashells.
Circle stones around.
Place her in a silver box.
Lay her in the ground.
And it's sing all you children, sing this song.
Sing all you children, sing.
Sing along.

A few weeks later, Leo's Mom calls him over to sit on her lap. She says, "Leo, I have something important to tell you. Your Nana is very sick. She will be taking powerful medicine to help her get better." Leo begins to cry. "Will I never have another play day with Nana? I will miss her so much!"

"You don't have to worry, Leo. Today is your play day with Nana. Sometimes your play days will have to be quiet because Nana's medicine will make her tired. You can read books, draw, or play games together as Nana rests. Sometimes Gramps will take you outside for fun adventures when Nana needs to sleep."

"Some play days will be busy when Nana's medicine is working, and she is less tired. You can bake cookies, go on short walks, or play catch."

One day, Leo finds Nana lying on the sofa with NO HAIR! There is a stack of fancy hats on the table next to her. Leo shouts, "Nana, where is your hair?" Nana laughs and says, "My medicine made my hair fall out. It will grow back."

Nana asks Leo to pick out the hat she will wear for the day.

Over the course of the year, Leo and Nana have many quiet play days and some busy play days. Eventually, they find out the medicine is no longer working. Nana's body becomes weaker and weaker. Mostly, play days are with Gramps, while Nana rests.

As time passes, Nana has to stay in bed. Leo's family creates a special room with a hospital bed to make Nana comfortable. It is filled with flowers and soft music. Hospice ladies come to help Leo and his family say goodbye. One morning, Nana isn't talking, she isn't eating and she isn't moving. Leo says, "It is like the little bird. Nana's TWINKLE is gone." The family cries and hugs each other. Nana will be so missed.

The next week, a funeral is held for Nana. Before everyone arrives for the service, Leo draws a heart picture. On it he writes, "I love you, Nana. I will miss you forever." He cries softly and says goodbye. His heart hurts so much. He feels as if it will break. Nana's body is inside a silver box called a casket. Leo places the picture inside the box. Leo and his Mom have a long, tender hug.

During the funeral, Nana's silver box is placed in the center of a huge room. There are beautiful flowers, and her favorite music is playing. Special friends and family tell stories and say nice things about Nana. There are lots of tears and some laughter too.

After the funeral service, Leo's family goes to the
cemetery. Nana's silver box is placed into a grave. Leo
and his family put lots of flowers on top of the casket.
Leo's Mom tells him that a special stone is being made
to put on the grave to mark Nana's spot. It is called a
headstone. The family cries and says goodbye.

Leo and his family go back to Nana and Gramps' house. Nana said she wanted a "party" after she died. There is delicious food, music, photographs of Nana with friends and family, and flowers of all kinds. Leo is feeling sad, but he also feels some relief that Nana's party is just what she wished for.

During the party, Leo's Mom bends down and whispers in his ear. She asks, "Leo, where do you think Nana's TWINKLE has gone?"

Leo takes his Mom's hand and leads her outside into the night. The sky is filled with bright stars. Leo points to the biggest and brightest star.

He says, "There is Nana's TWINKLE!"

GLOSSARY

BODY – what is left after a person dies. Remember that a dead body is just a shell. For Leo, the body is what remains when the TWINKLE is gone.

CASKET – a box where the dead body is placed before it is buried.

CELEBRATION OF LIFE – a gathering of family and friends who share memories and how grateful they are that the person who has died "lived." In this story, Nana wanted her celebration to be a "party."

CEMETERY – a place where the bodies of people who have died are buried.

CONDOLENCES – telling a grieving person that you are sad about their loss. "Condolence" means giving comfort through words we say, sympathy cards, flowers, etc.

CREMATION – when a dead body is turned to ash. The body is turned to ash through burning. The dead feel no pain. The ashes are often put into an urn or other container. Some people scatter the ashes over a favorite place that their loved one requests. Some people bury the urn or keep it in a special place in the cemetery.

DEAD – when the body stops working. Leo believes that dead means that the TWINKLE is gone from the body. Some people call the TWINKLE the soul, spirit, or life force.

FUNERAL – a time after a person has died when family, friends, and neighbors come together to say goodbye, share special memories about the person's life, and offer condolences.

GRAVE - the hole in which the casket is placed in the cemetery. It is covered with dirt, and often flowers are placed on top.

HEADSTONE - a carved stone that marks the grave, so that everyone will know who is buried there. Sometimes headstones are called markers.

HOSPICE - a program that provides special care for people who are near the end of life. Hospice can be provided at home, a hospital or another special designated place.

HELPING CHILDREN DEAL WITH GRIEF

Each child's grief process is unique. Their developmental age will determine how they are able to handle death and grief. This book is written for children between the ages of 5 and 9 years. At this stage in their development, children are transitioning in their grasp of what it means to die. They are moving from the 3 - 5-year-old stage of "magical thinking." From 3 - 5 years, they often believe that the dead person will return, or somehow the death was their fault. For instance, the child may think, "Because I once was angry with Nana, she became sick and died." However, between 5 and 9 years of age, there is generally the realization that the person who died is not coming back and that they did not cause the death. In this book, Leo uses "magical thinking" to explain what it means to be dead. He describes death as when the TWINKLE is gone.

Leo also uses "magical thinking" to describe where Nana is now. He points to the heavens and he sees her as a shining star. He knows she will not return, but this perception obviously comforts him. Each child and each adult develops their own perception of what death means, and it is in our struggle through our process of grief that we are able to come to some acceptance of the natural cycle of life and death.

Your child may ask the same questions over and over again. Children are naturally curious about death, even before they experience a personal loss. The same questions may be asked over a period of weeks and months. It is difficult for a child to understand everything at once. A child may be attempting through repetition to work through his/her grief. As children mature emotionally and intellectually, the information and the answers you provide can become more meaningful. Using the seasons or the natural life cycle of living things can be helpful for children to understand death in a real and meaningful way. Walks in nature can provide much fuel for understanding life and death.

It is important not to avoid using the word "death." When referring to the deceased, do not use phrases such as "gone away," "lost," or "went to sleep." This can create confusion in the younger child, and give older children the impression that death is something to be feared and not to be discussed.

Be honest with your child. They will ask you if you are going to die? Will I die? Who will take care of me? etc. Just answer these questions as truthfully, clearly and age appropriately as you can. In response to whether she or dad could die, one mother said, "I told him it is extremely unlikely that we will die soon. We are healthy and young, and we are super careful about not putting

ourselves in danger. But I didn't say no, we won't die. I knew that lying would have led to distrust when he found out the truth." These questions about death offer us the opportunity to discuss the natural cycle of life and death. All living creatures have their time to live and their time to die.

Grief can take time, and expect varying degrees of emotion. Grieving is a process, not an event. There is no "correct" way to move through the grieving process. Respect your child's process. Your child may seem nonchalant about the death and then suddenly fall apart over a broken toy. Children will often cry, express sadness and then suddenly be off running and playing. Grief often comes in waves. When another wave comes, it might overwhelm your child with anger or

fear. Some children may regress, become more clingy, or want to come into your bed. Do not hide your own feelings. Let your child know that it's okay to cry and be sad over someone you love. You will be teaching him/her how to handle grief in a healthy way.

Your child needs you more than ever when you are experiencing intense feelings about the death of a loved one or friend. Children often feel ignored or invisible after there has been a death, especially if the loved one is a parent or someone with whom the child was close. Adults can be so caught up in their own grief that they do not realize how important it is to keep the children close. Even if you are attempting to shelter them from the sorrow, children sense the feelings anyway. They need to have more attention at this time. Include them in the planning of the funeral or memorial as much as possible. Just keep them close. It is healthy to strengthen your bonds and connection at these difficult times of goodbye.

Consider taking your child to the funeral or memorial. It used to be that parents often wanted to shield their children from the pain and sadness of the goodbyes. However, the newest research shows that the funeral is a "rite of separation." It helps us face the reality of death. It is an important aspect of our children's process of grieving and healing.

In this book, Leo attends his Nana's funeral service, her burial and the "party" that celebrates her life. Prior to her death, he was present over the course of a year as her illness made her weaker and weaker. He was even present as the TWINKLE left her body. Of course individual decisions will have to be made as to which part of the grief process your child should be part of. I believe that the 5 - 9-year-olds this book is written for should be included as much as possible. You can explain

to your child what happens at a funeral. If your child objects to attending, you need not force him/her to go. I have found that most children want to be part of the process in some way.

Develop some rituals with your child. Rituals are usually something we do over and over again. Rituals can provide remembering, comfort, acceptance, and healing. Some examples of rituals are:

-Placing flowers on the grave at special times like birthdays, anniversaries, or Memorial Day.
-Drawing pictures to place inside the coffin or on the grave.
-Playing special music, looking at photographs, and reading or saying special things about the deceased loved one or friend on their birthday or the anniversary of their death.
-On special holidays, take time for each person to say one thing that they remember about the deceased. Each person can light a candle in remembrance of the loved one or friend.
-Be creative and think of your own rituals. Allow your child to contribute suggestions. The more included your child feels, the more his/her loss will feel understood.

If there has been a traumatic death such as the suicide of a loved one or friend, your child may have a difficult time moving through the grief process. Seeking professional grief counseling can be helpful in dealing with traumatic experiences.

RESOURCES

www.dougy.org
help@dougy.org
PO Box 86852
Portland, OR
(503) 775-5683
Toll free (866) 775-5683

www.healingcenterseattle.org
6409 ½ Roosevelt Way NE
Seattle, WA 98115
(206) 523-1206

www.hellogrief.org

www.naeyc.org/resources/pubs/tyc/jun2009/childrens-books-death
(Children's Books about Death)

www.childrengrieve.org

"The Little Bird Is Dead" – Song in the book WHEN THE TWINKLE
IS GONE. On the CD "Spin Spider Spin" by Patty Zeitlin and Marcia
Berman

BEVERLY CUEVAS, AUTHOR

Beverly has been a clinical social worker specializing in issues of attachment, trauma, and grief over 45 years. She is a founding member of ATTAch (The Association for Training on Trauma and Attachment in Children). She has presented workshops on attachment and grief throughout the country. This book reflects her respect for a child's perspective in dealing with loss, death, and grief. It highlights the ability of children to understand the natural cycle of life and death. Beverly says, "The children have taught me so much about the acceptance of 'what is' in life including the acceptance of its ending."

Beverly is a wife, mother and grandmother. She lives with her husband in Seattle, WA. She continues a therapeutic practice in Kirkland, WA.

PAULA PUGH, ILLUSTRATOR

Paula is an author (Celebrating Beginnings and Endings), violinist, personal journal artist, grandmother, boater, wife and mother. Helping children understand that death is a natural part of life, and how they can be active and present in the process, warms her heart. She lives on an island in the Salish Sea with her husband and fuzzy dog.